Contents

KT-525-291

Words that are highlighted can be found in the glossary.

What is football?

The modern, international **game we know as football has come a long way from its early days.**

Modern-day Cuju festival.

The first known sport that was anything like football was called Cuju. Cuju was played in China in the second century and involved kicking balls stuffed with feathers.

Modern-day mob football festival.

Early football in **medieval** Europe was called mob football. Whole villages fought to get the ball to each others' market places – there were no other rules!

GT Top Fact

Main rules of modern football:
• two teams of 11 players play for 90 minutes, which is split into two 45-minute halves
• the teams try to score more goals than each other by getting the ball into the other team's goal.

 How many international football **strips** can you identify on the pages of this book?

Football pitch

Football is played on a pitch which is no more than 120 metres (m) long and 90m wide. Each team defends their half of the pitch and attacks their opponent's half.

Pitch conditions can change during rain and other weather.

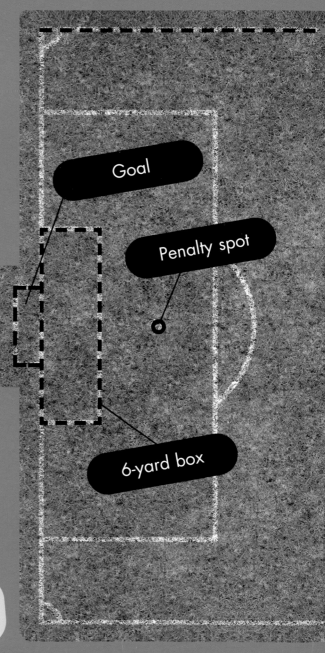

Goal

Penalty spot

6-yard box

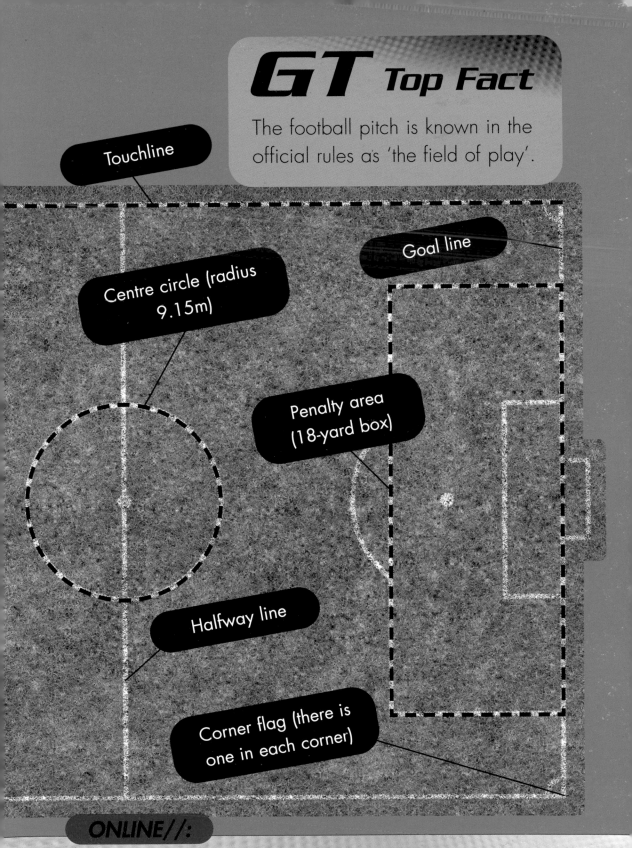

GT Top Fact

The football pitch is known in the official rules as 'the field of play'.

Touchline

Goal line

Centre circle (radius 9.15m)

Penalty area (18-yard box)

Halfway line

Corner flag (there is one in each corner)

ONLINE//:

http://www.fifa.com/classicfootball/stadiums
Visit this section of the FIFA website and find out more about the
classic stadiums of the world.

Go professional

It takes a lot of skill and hard work to become a professional **footballer. Many players don't make it, but these five steps might help. Who knows, maybe someone reading this book will become a professional player.**

Theo Walcott (right) played for England when he was 17 years and 75 days old.

1. Play football as much as you can – with friends, or family, or on your own.

2. Join a local team. If you need advice in finding a good one, visit the website of FIFA (see opposite).

GT Record

Arsenal are the best women's football team in England. They have won 10 out of 16 **league championships**.

GT Top Fact

Germany won the women's World Cup in 2007 held in China (below). They beat Brazil 2–0.

ONLINE//:

http://ussoccer.com

This is the website of the US **Soccer** Federation, featuring women's team news, photos and videos. Also features the men's soccer team.

Europe's greatest teams

Twelve teams have won the Champions League (or European Cup) more than once. Teams from Spain, Italy and England have dominated the tournament since it began in 1955.

In 2001 Liverpool won three competitions: the Champions League, the FA Cup and the League (Premier) Cup.

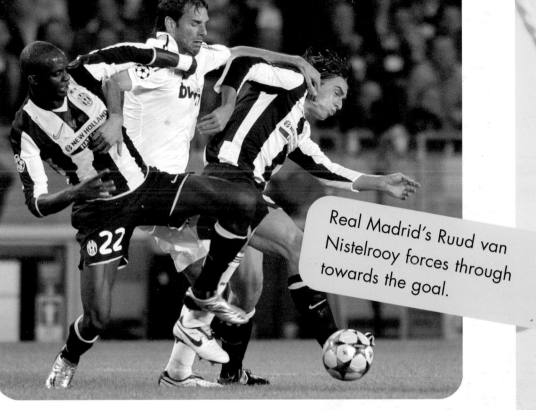

Real Madrid's Ruud van Nistelrooy forces through towards the goal.

Go Turbo Winners

Champions League winners

Teams	Wins	Teams	Wins
Real Madrid	9	Barcelona	2
AC Milan	7	Benfica	2
Liverpool	5	FC Porto	2
Ajax Amsterdam	4	Inter Milan	2
Bayern Munich	4	Juventus	2
Manchester United	3	Nottingham Forest	2

ONLINE//:

http://www.uefa.com/competitions/ucl
Visit these UEFA webpages for the Champions League to swot up
on the League's history, statistics, clubs and current standings.

FIFA World Cup

The World Cup is the ultimate
 ootball tournament. It takes place
every four years. Countries from
six continents **play each other to**
qualify, **with most teams coming**
 rom Europe and South America.

GT Top Fact

Brazil is the only team to win the World
Cup when it has been held outside their
own continent: 1958 (above) in Europe and
2002 in Japan. No European team has
ever won the tournament away from Europe.

Marco Materazzi of Italy heads the ball towards the goal during the 2006 World Cup Final.

Countries qualify for the World Cup finals by playing other teams from their part of the world. Teams that have qualified go to the World Cup finals.

204 countries entered to take part in the 2010 World Cup. When the finals take place only 30 teams will be left.

The current World Cup trophy is the second trophy to be used. Brazil was given the original Jules Rimet trophy to keep after winning the tournament for the third time in 1970. A new trophy was introduced in 1974 and it is still used today.

GT Record

Only seven countries have ever won the trophy. Brazil have won it the most times: five.

Go Turbo Winners

World Cup winners

1930	Uruguay
1934	Italy
1938	Italy
1950	Uruguay
1954	West Germany
1958	Brazil
1962	Brazil
1966	England
1970	Brazil
1974	West Germany
1978	Argentina
1982	Italy
1986	Argentina
1990	West Germany
1994	Brazil
1998	France
2002	Brazil
2006	Italy

The current World Cup trophy weighs 6.2 kilograms and is 35.56 centimetres high.

 The World Cup is played every four years. Why wasn't it played between 1938 and 1950?

ONLINE//:

http://www.fifa.com/worldcup/index.html
Find out more about the World Cup, including its history, photos, team lists and statistics.

Football records

The first football club formed in Sheffield, England in 1857. Since then records have been set and broken, including: highest scores; biggest attendances; most international appearances.

These are some of the most amazing records.
Choose below from either answer A, B or C.
The actual answers are on page 43 – no cheating!

? **1.** Dixie Dean scored the most goals in one season in English football. (Everton, 1927–1928). In 39 games how many goals did he score?
A: 40, B: 50 or C: 60

 2. Egypt have appeared in the final of the African Cup of Nations more than any other team. But how many times? A: 3, B: 5 or C: 9

 3. The 1950 Brazil–Uruguay World Cup final had the world's biggest attendance at a football game. How many people were there? A: 104,113, B: 154,915 or C: 199,850

ONLINE//:

http://news.bbc.co.uk/sport1/hi/football/world_cup_200 6/video_archive/default.stm   Watch archive videos of past World Cup games and find out about the Brazil-Uruguay match.

How to take the perfect penalty

A penalty is awarded to a team if their opponents commit a foul, such as a handball, in the penalty area.

GT Top Fact

The first ever penalty kick was awarded to Wolverhampton Wanderers against Accrington Stanley in 1891. They scored.

Ghanaian players practise taking penalty kicks.

Researchers at Liverpool John Moores University have found out four steps to take the perfect penalty – Chelsea's John Terry (below, centre) might want to know these. He missed a penalty in the 2008 Champions' League Final.

Go Turbo Skill

1. Practise taking penalties as often as you can.
2. Just do it – do not think too deeply.
3. Strike the ball hard.
4. Aim for one of the top corners.
5. Smile at the goalkeeper before you shoot.*

*we added this one – it works for us!

ONLINE//:

http://news.bbc.co.uk/sport1/hi/football/skills
This webpage is part of the BBC's sports pages. It features skills videos, step-by-step instructions and masterclasses from top players.

Football rich list

For most fans, football is simply about their team winning. But football is a multi-million pound business.

Top football clubs can earn hundreds of millions of pounds through ticket income, shirt sales and selling rights to TV and sponsors.

Every year a company called Deloitte publishes a list of the richest football clubs in the world. It tells you how much each club earns.

Go Turbo Rich List

The top five in 2008:

1	Real Madrid	£236.2 million
2	Manchester United	£212.1 million
3	Barcelona	£195.3 million
4	Chelsea	£190.5 million
5	Arsenal	£177.6 million

GT Top Fact

Real Madrid's Bernabeu stadium (shown here) holds 80,000 people.

ONLINE//:

http://www.realmadrid.com
Homepage of the richest football club in the world: Real Madrid. Catch up with the latest team news, photos and videos.

Different games

Around the world there are lots of other ways football is played.

Beach soccer is more than just a group of friends playing at the seaside. It has its own rules, which include players not wearing shoes. Beach soccer is famous as the sport where Brazilian players become so skilful.

Futsal is an indoor version of five-a-side football. There are no walls or boards at the side of the pitch, as in some five-a-side versions of the game. The ball is smaller than a normal football and has less bounce.

The Brazilian futsal team in action.

These girls are beach soccer training in Rio de Janeiro, Brazil.

Powerchair football is played by two teams of four people in wheelchairs. The players use footguards to kick the larger than normal ball up and down the pitch. Powerchair football has its own world cup.

ONLINE//:

http://www.thewfa.org.uk
Home of the Wheelchair Football Association. Find out about the clubs, leagues and get up-to-date news.

Hot Wheels

Written by Leon Read

Illustrated by Kevin Hopgood

I'm outside on the school five-a-side football pitch. My friends are passing the ball around. Sometimes I get the ball, especially if they don't hear me coming – my powerchair motors are almost silent. They don't tackle me because I'll run over their feet.

The school sport's coach is watching me.

Yes, I am in a powerchair. OK, so it's really cool – a Storm X – but there's no need to stare. The coach walks over.

"Hi!" he says, trying to look cool talking to the disabled kid. "Wes, right? I'm Dennis. That was some fancy ball work."

"What, for a kid in a chair?" I snap.

"That wasn't really what I meant. They are some really hot wheels. A Storm X, isn't it?"

That freaks me out a bit. "Yeah. How come you know so much?"

"I'm the Power Sharks coach – the powerchair football team."

"What? Whoever heard of powerchair football? What a stupid idea."

"It's just football. Listen, Wes, we've got a training session here tomorrow. You should come along."

I tell him I'll think about it.

After school the next day, I decide to ride over to the indoor five-a-side pitch. Inside it smells of sweat. The sound of lots of voices freaks me out a bit. Dennis waves when he sees me.

"Hey, Wes!" he says. "Let me introduce you to the team."

He fits my chair with a bumper and it helps me to control the ball. I can spin round and strike the ball hard.

Dennis explains the rules. A match is 40 minutes long. There are eight players on each side, but only four of them can be on the pitch, and one must be the goalkeeper. There are unlimited substitutions.

There's a match at the weekend. Dennis says I can play.

Saturday comes at last. There are lots of people at the pitch and there's so much noise. But I must stay calm.

The referee blows his whistle and the game starts, but I'm not on the pitch! I'm a substitute.

I start to feel angry. Mum said I must not get too excited, so I try to remember that. Except in two minutes we are losing 0–2!

We get to half-time and the score is still 0–2.

Finally, I'm on! But the other team keep stealing the ball from my bumper. I ram one of their players, and give away a free kick. Then they go and score, now it's 0–3. Dennis gives me his calm down signal.

Now there are just five minutes left. Shaun has scored twice for us, so it's 2–3. But time is running out! I'm playing better now. I pass the ball to Shaun and he controls it. We zoom forward quickly. I'm in the penalty area.

"Shaun, over here!" He passes just before he is blocked. The ball rolls to my bumper. I spin, then shoot. The goalkeeper tries to block the ball, but it's going too fast. Goal!

Shaun comes over and we high-five. He can't talk well, but he gives me a big thumbs up and smiles. Now it's 3–3.

The match finishes 3–3 – but it feels like we have won. Dennis says there is still work to do, but that I could be part of a really good team.

Football Fitness

As well as training and keeping fit, footballers have to eat well and live a healthy lifestyle.

Amateur and professional players often have diet sheets. These show the players what they should and should not eat. Players are encouraged to drink water regularly and not to smoke or drink alcohol.

A footballer's professional career may only last 10–15 years. It is important to stay fit, especially as players get older, so they can play at the top level.

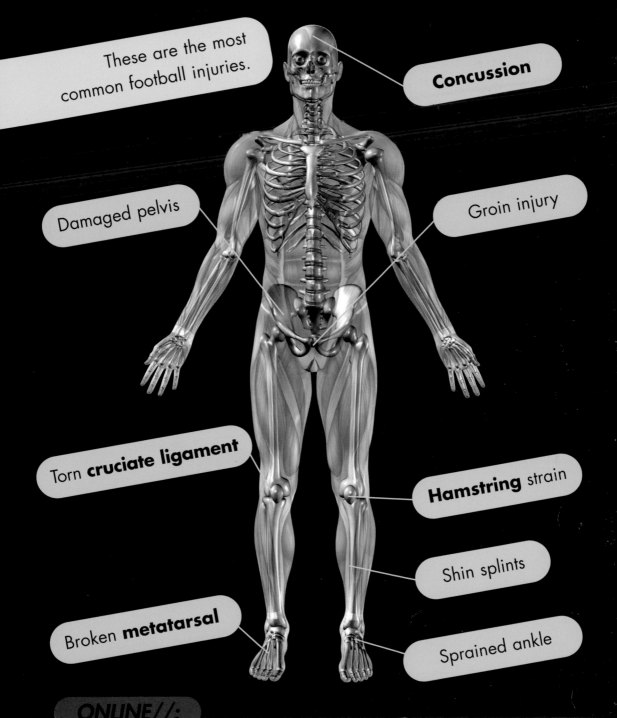

These are the most common football injuries.

Concussion

Damaged pelvis

Groin injury

Torn **cruciate ligament**

Hamstring strain

Shin splints

Broken **metatarsal**

Sprained ankle

ONLINE//:

http://www.thefa.com/GrassrootsNew/Player/Postings/ 2004/03/FootballNutrition
Get the latest football food news on this FA 'Food for thought' webpage.

The original 12

Twelve clubs have the honour of being the original founding members of the English football league in 1888. But where were they in 2008–2009?

Premiership
Aston Villa
Blackburn Rovers
Bolton Wanderers
Everton
Stoke
West Bromwich Albion

Championship
Burnley
Derby County
Preston North End
Wolverhampton
 Wanderers

League Two
Accrington Stanley
Notts County

This is the Aston Villa team that won the FA Cup in 1913.

GT Top Fact

Of the original 12 teams, Everton has been the most successful winning the league title nine times. Aston Villa has won it seven times.

Wolverhampton Wanderers celebrate promotion to the Premiership in 2003.

 Do you know which of the 12 clubs is the oldest? Search online (see below) to find out which team won the first English Championship.

ONLINE//:

http://www.nationalfootballmuseum.com
Website of the National Football Museum, where you can find out how football strips have changed, and follow a key dates timeline.

Who's best?

Two people are usually considered the best footballers ever: Pelé, from Brazil, and Diego Maradona, from Argentina.

There is little to tell them apart. They shared the FIFA Footballer of the Century award. The experts can't agree who is the best, some choose Pelé, others choose Maradona.

Pelé in action in 1960.

Why don't you make up your own mind.
Here are some statistics about their careers:

	Pelé (Brazil)	Maradona (Argentina)
Age at national **debut**	16	16
Club games	468	590
Club goals	501	331
National games	92	91
National goals	77	34
World Cup wins	3	1
Club trophies	25	10

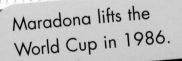

Maradona lifts the World Cup in 1986.

 Some people think Maradona does not deserve to be called the best footballer because he has been banned for taking drugs. What do you think?

Some people in countries such as the USA and Australia call football 'soccer'. Soccer comes from the phrase 'association football'.

Jim Fryatt scored the fastest goal in league history in 1964 – at just 4 seconds!

Some people believe that the first football club was formed in Edinburgh, Scotland, in 1824.

The record score in a UK football match is Arbroath 36, Bon Accord 0 in the Scottish FA Cup.

An inflated pig's bladder was originally used as the ball for mob football. Some people said that before the bladder they used a dead soldier's head.

Arthur Rowley scored the most English league goals. From 1946–1965, he scored 433 goals in 619 games.

Answers

Page 7: 16 international strips: (p.8 Chile and Italy),
(p.10 Kazakhstan and England), (p.11 Northern Ireland and
Yugoslavia), (p.13 Portugal), (p.14 The USA and Germany),
(p.18 Brazil), (p.19 France), (p.23 Cameroon, Egypt and
Uruguay), *(p.24 Ghana, but you can't really see the strip,
so it doesn't count)*, (p.28 Ukraine), (p.41 Argentina).

Page 13: The answer to this question will depend on your
own opinion. Find out what your friends think – their opinion
might depend on the football team that they support.

Page 14: The football authorities believed women were
better off at home, where they could look after their families.

Page 21: World War II (1939–1945) meant that football
could not be played.

Pages 22 and 23: 1=C, 2=B, 3=C.

Page 39: Preston North End is the oldest of the clubs.

Page 41: The answer to this question will depend on your
own opinion. Try discussing the question with your friends to
find out what they think.

More websites

This is the website of the Federation of Futsal USA, featuring a history of the game, rules, videos and a photo gallery:

http://fefusa.zortal.com

Home of the Football Federation Australia, featuring news about the men's and women's teams:

www.footballaustralia. com.au

Website from Beach Soccer Worldwide, featuring the latest competition news and beach soccer videos:

www.beachsoccer.com

UEFA.com magazine, with all the latest news, podcasts and videos from across Europe:

www1.uefa.com/maga zine/index2.html

Website of one of the most famous football clubs in the world – Manchester United:

www.manutd.com

Powerchair Football International Federation website, with international team news, videos, photo galleries and sport history:

www.fipfa.org

Watch a video featuring football legend, Jack Charlton, and the Percy Hedley Sports Academy powerchair football team:

www.percyhedley.org. uk/media/powerchair. mpg

The on-line home of football in New Zealand, includes news and team fixture information:

www.nzsoccer.com

Glossary

Amateur – not professional. In football this means a player has another job because he or she does not get paid for playing football.

Classic – something that is considered to be a great example and very important.

Concussion – the effects on the body after being knocked out.

Continent – one of the seven large land areas in the world.

Cruciate ligament – cross-shaped band in the knee.

Debut – the first time something or someone appears in a particular place.

Dominated – to have been the most successful at something for a period of time.

Hamstring – a tendon at the back of the knee.

International – something that occurs across the world, in many different nations.

League championships – a type of competition in which teams play against each other. Scores are recorded in tables.

Medieval – relating to the period of history called the Middle Ages (c.476CE to 1453).

Metatarsal – any of the five long bones in the foot.

Original – the first, or earliest to exist.

Professional – not amateur. In football this means that players are paid to play football, so they can spend all their time practising their skills.

Qualify – in football, to be entered into a competition after winning specific football matches.

Soccer – the name given to football in many parts of the English-speaking world, especially in the USA and Australia. See fact on page 42.

Strips – the team kits worn by footballers and other sportspeople.

V. – the abbreviation of 'versus', which means to compete against.

Index